*To the
great, grand,
and goofy
Griffin family.*

Contents

1

Gaylord & Gladys Goofy

Gaylord: Who delivers breakfast, lunch, and dinner and always completes his appointed rounds?
Gladys: Beats me.
Gaylord: The mealman.

Gaylord: Why do thermometers go to school?
Gladys: I can't guess.
Gaylord: To earn their degrees.

Gaylord: Why couldn't the geometry teacher walk?
Gladys: I have no idea.
Gaylord: He had a sprained angle.

Gaylord: What do you get if you cross two insects and a rabbit?

Gladys: I don't know.
Gaylord: Bugs Bunny.

Gaylord: What state is a number?
Gladys: I have know idea.
Gaylord: Tenn.

Gaylord: What's red, white, and blue, and
handy if you sneeze?
Gladys: You tell me.
Gaylord: Hanky Doodle Dandy.

Gaylord: What's stingy, hates Christmas,
and lays eggs?
Gladys: I give up.
Gaylord: Ebenezer Chicken.

Gaylord: What is big and yellow and
comes in the morning to brighten
Mother's day?
Gladys: Who knows?
Gaylord: The school bus.

Gaylord: What do you say to a hitchhiking
frog?
Gladys: You've got me.

Gaylord: Hop in!

⚜

Gaylord: What would you get if you blew
    your hair dryer down a rabbit hole?
Gladys: My mind is a blank.
Gaylord: Hot cross bunnies.

⚜

Gaylord: What do you say to Emillion
    when he does you a good turn?
Gladys: That's a mystery.
Gaylord: Thanks, Emillion.

⚜

Gaylord: What is gray on the inside and
    clear on the outside?
Gladys: Tell me.
Gaylord: An elephant in a Baggie.

⚜

Gaylord: What always speaks the truth
    but doesn't say a word?
Gladys: I don't have the foggiest.
Gaylord: A mirror.

⚜

Gaylord: What do you get if you cross an
    owl with an oyster?
Gladys: It's unknown to me.

Gaylord: An animal that drops pearls of wisdom.

2

Gertrude & Gerard Goofy

Gertrude: Who has six legs, wears a
  coonskin cap, and chirps?
Gerard: Beats me.
Gertrude: Davy Cricket.

Gertrude: Why shouldn't you ever give
  your heart to a tennis player?
Gerard: I can't guess.
Gertrude: Because to him, love means
  nothing.

Gertrude: Why did the teeny-bopper hold
  a stone up to her left ear and a
  hamburger bun up to her right ear?
Gerard: I have no idea.
Gertrude: Because she wanted to hear
  rock-and-roll.

Gertrude: What did the chewing gum say to the shoe?
Gerard: I don't know.
Gertrude: I'm stuck on you.

Gertrude: What Arizona city is named for a banner pole?
Gerard: I have know idea.
Gertrude: Flagstaff.

Gertrude: What's easier to give than to receive?
Gerard: You tell me.
Gertrude: Criticism.

Gertrude: What did the tree surgeon say to the diseased dogwood?
Gerard: I give up.
Gertrude: Your bark is worse than your blight.

Gertrude: What shoes should you wear when your basement is flooded?
Gerard: Who knows?
Gertrude: Pumps.

Gertrude: What singing grasshopper lives
  in a fireplace?
Gerard: You've got me.
Gertrude: Chimney Cricket.

Gertrude: What is a fish's favorite game?
Gerard: My mind is a blank.
Gertrude: Salmon Says.

Gertrude: What is a thief's favorite game?
Gerard: That's a mystery.
Gertrude: Hide 'n sneak.

Gertrude: What family car doesn't move?
Gerard: Tell me.
Gertrude: A stationary wagon.

Gertrude: What do frogs drink at snack
  time?
Gerard: I don't have the foggiest
Gertrude: Croak-a-Cola.

Gertrude: What kind of geese are found in
   Portugal?
Gerard: It's unknown to me.
Gertrude: Portu-geese.

3
Gus & Gabriel Goofy

Gus: Who is the nastiest Disney
character?
Gabriel: Beats me.
Gus: Meanie Mouse.

Gus: Why did the paintbrush retire?
Gabriel: I can't guess.
Gus: It had a stroke.

Gus: Why did the umpire throw the
chicken out of the baseball game?
Gabriel: I have no idea.
Gus: He suspected fowl play.

Gus: What do you get from a dog and a
chicken combined?
Gabriel: I don't know.
Gus: A pooched egg.

Gus: What is a cat with a lemon?
Gabriel: I have no idea.
Gus: A sour puss.

Gus: What do you get if you have an
  elephant with a jar of peanut butter?
Gabriel: You tell me.
Gus: You either get peanut butter with a
  wonderful memory or an elephant
  that sticks to the roof of your mouth.

Gus: What kind of music can you play
  with a shoehorn?
Gabriel: I give up.
Gus: Footnotes.

Gus: What's a liar's favorite month?
Gabriel: Who knows?
Gus: Fibruary.

Gus: What kind of shot do you give a sick
  car?
Gabriel: You've got me.
Gus: A fuel injection.

Gus: What does the government use when
it takes a census of all the monkeys in
the zoos?
Gabriel: My mind is a blank.
Gus: An ape recorder.

Gus: What are the last three hairs on a
dog's tail called?
Gabriel: That's a mystery.
Gus: Dog hairs.

Gus: What is black and white and has 16
wheels?
Gabriel: Tell me.
Gus: A zebra on roller skates.

Gus: What do hippopotamuses have that
no other animal has?
Gabriel: It's unknown to me.
Gus: Baby hippopotamuses.

4

Goofy Guffaws!

Have you ever seen a horse fly?

Have you ever seen an egg box?

A catty remark often has more lives than a cat.

"My business is for the birds," said the goofy pet store owner.

Why hasn't someone invented black light bulbs for people who want to read in the dark?

The goofy garbage man once wrote a novel. It made the best-smeller list.

Did you hear about the goofy dentist?
He thought he had a lot of pull.

You tell 'em, clock, you've got the time.

In a car wash: Grime Does Not Pay.

You tell 'em, cashier, I'm a poor teller.

You tell 'em, hunter, I'm game.

You tell 'em, Simon, I'll Legree.

"My business is down in the dumps," said
    the garbage man.

5

Geraldine & Gaspar Goofy

Geraldine: Who are the most despised
 football players?
Gaspar: Beats me.
Geraldine: The offensive team.

Geraldine: Why do golfers wear two pairs
 of pants?
Gaspar: I can't guess.
Geraldine: In case they get a hole in one.

Geraldine: Why do lions roar?
Gasper: I have no idea.
Geraldine: They would feel silly saying
 oink, oink.

Geraldine: What amusement park ride is
 only 12 inches long?

Gasper: I don't know.
Geraldine: A ruler coaster.

Geraldine: What nut is like a sneeze?
Gasper: I have no idea.
Geraldine: A cashew.

Geraldine: What does a kid need if he's
    absent from school during final
    exams?
Gasper: You tell me.
Geraldine: A good excuse.

Geraldine: What vitamin has good vision?
Gasper: I give up.
Geraldine: Vitamin C.

Geraldine: What do you get when you
    cross an elephant with a Volkswagon?
Gasper: Who knows?
Geraldine: A little car with a big trunk.

Geraldine: What did the silly comedian
    bake on his day off?
Gasper: You've got me.
Geraldine: Corn bread.

Geraldine: What do you get when you
cross a stream and a brook?
Gasper: My mind is a blank.
Geraldine: Wet feet.

Geraldine: What use is a reindeer?
Gasper: That's a mystery.
Geraldine: It makes the flowers grow,
sweetie.

Geraldine: What do magicians say on
Halloween?
Gasper: Tell me.
Geraldine: Trick-or-trick?

Geraldine: What kind of lizard loves
riddles?
Gasper: I don't have the foggiest.
Geraldine: A sillymander.

Geraldine: What is the strangest kind of
commercial?
Gasper: It's unknown to me.
Geraldine: An oddvertisement.

6
Gideon & Gloria Goofy

Gideon: Who does Clark Kent turn into
  when he's hungry?
Gloria: Beats me.
Gideon: Supperman.

Gideon: Why did the farmer get a ticket?
Gloria: I can't guess.
Gideon: He exceeded the seed limit.

Gideon: Why did the swimmer get a
  ticket?
Gloria: I have no idea.
Gideon: He was caught diving without a
  license.

Gideon: What dog do you find at the
  U.N.?
Gloria: I don't know.

Gideon: A diplomutt.

⚜

Gideon: What big cat lives in the
    backyard?
Gloria: I have no idea.
Gideon: A clotheslion.

⚜

Gideon: What happened when the cat
    swallowed a ball of yarn?
Gloria: You tell me.
Gideon: She had mittens.

⚜

Gideon: What is a minister doing when he
    rehearses his sermon?
Gloria: I give up.
Gideon: Practicing what he preaches.

⚜

Gideon: What do you call the boss at a
    dairy?
Gloria: Who knows?
Gideon: The big cheese.

⚜

Gideon: What do you call it when five
    toads sit on top of each other?
Gloria: You've got me.
Gideon: A toad-em pole.

Gideon: What music do steel workers play
    at their parties?
Gloria: My mind is a blank.
Gideon: Heavy metal.

Gideon: What school do dogs go to?
Gloria: That's a mystery.
Gideon: Barkley.

Gideon: What is a mouse's favorite game?
Gloria: Tell me.
Gideon: Hide 'n squeak.

Gideon: What do you get if you tie two
    bicycles together?
Gloria: I don't have the foggiest.
Gideon: Siamese Schwinns.

Gideon: What is the funniest car on the
    road?
Gloria: It's unknown to me.
Gideon: A Jolkswagen.

7

Gwendolyn & Godfrey Goofy

Gwendolyn: Who carries a basket, visits
  Grandma, and steals jewelry?
Godfrey: Beats me.
Gwendolyn: Little Red Robin Hood.

Gwendolyn: Why was the baseball player
  asked to come on the camping trip?
Godfrey: I can't guess.
Gwendolyn: They needed someone to
  pitch the tent.

Gwendolyn: Why is it hard to drive a golf
  ball?
Godfrey: I have no idea.
Gwendolyn: Because it doesn't have a
  steering wheel.

Gwendolyn: What cereal goes snap, crackle, squeak?
Godfrey: I don't know.
Gwendolyn: Mice Krispies.

Gwendolyn: What did the parrot say to the streetcar?
Godfrey: I have no idea.
Gwendolyn: Trolley want a cracker?

Gwendolyn: What do you get if you cross bubble gum, a hen, and a dog?
Godfrey: You tell me.
Gwendolyn: Snap, cackle and pup.

Gwendolyn: What has big eyes, green skin, and lives alone?
Godfrey: I give up.
Gwendolyn: Hermit the Frog.

Gwendolyn: What's big and white and scores a lot of strikes?
Godfrey: Who knows?
Gwendolyn: A bowler bear.

Gwendolyn: What does Sherlock Holmes read for fun?
Godfrey: You've got me.
Gwendolyn: The encycluepedia.

Gwendolyn: What do you get when you cross the United States and the United Kingdom?
Godfrey: My mind is a blank.
Gwendolyn: The Atlantic Ocean.

Gwendolyn: What American grasshopper likes to brave the frontier?
Godgrey: That's a mystery.
Gwendolyn: Davy Cricket.

Gwendolyn: What time is it when the kids need a nap?
Godfrey: Tell me.
Gwendolyn: Whine o'clock.

Gwendolyn: What does Sleeping Beauty gargle with?
Godfrey: I don't have the foggiest.
Gwendolyn: Rinse Charming.

Gwendolyn: What do you call a formal
   dance for turkeys.
Godfrey: It's unknown to me.
Gwendolyn: A turkey trot.

Gwendolyn: What did Mr. Bird call his
   son?
Godfrey: I'm in the dark.
Gwendolyn: A chirp off the old block.

8

Grover & Gretchen Goofy

Grover: Who invented the telephone and
is delicious with milk?
Gretchen: Beats me.
Grover: Alexander Graham Cracker.

Grover: Why did the rich lady buy a Ming
vase?
Gretchen: I can't guess.
Grover: To go with her Ming coat.

Grover: Why do elephants have ivory
tusks?
Gretchen: I have no idea.
Grover: Iron tusks would rust.

Grover: Why would a man in jail want to
catch the measles?

Gretchen: I don't know.
Grover: So he could break out.

Grover: What do you call a crazy chicken?
Gretchen: I have know idea.
Grover: A cuckoo cluck.

Grover: What bone can't a dog eat?
Gretchen: You tell me.
Grover: A trombone.

Grover: What do you get when you trip
    an elephant carrying a crate of
    oranges?
Gretchen: I give up.
Grover: Orange juice.

Grover: What's another name for a
    cowboy?
Gretchen: Who knows?
Grover: A bull.

Grover: What kind of bird eats the same
    worm eight times?
Gretchen: You've got me.
Grover: A swallow with the hiccups.

Grover: What do you do if there's a
kidnapping in Texas?
Gretchen: My mind is a blank.
Grover: Wake him up.

Grover: What does Mickey Mouse's
girlfriend wear?
Gretchen: That's a mystery.
Grover: Minnie skirts.

Grover: What is the world's slowest ship?
Gretchen: Tell me.
Grover: A snailboat.

Grover: What do you get if you cross a
skunk and a raccoon?
Gretchen: I don't have the foggiest.
Grover: A dirty look from the raccoon.

Grover: What happens when you ask an
oyster a personal question?
Gretchen: It's unknown to me.
Grover: It clams up.

Grover: What has wings, is out of its
    mind, and sits in trees?
Gretchen: I'm in the dark.
Grover: A raven lunatic.

9

Geneva & Guthrie Goofy

Geneva: Who rides in a sleigh, gives Christmas presents, and has many faults?
Guthrie: Beats me.
Geneva: Santa Flaws.

Geneva: Why should men avoid the letter A?
Guthrie: I can't guess.
Geneva: Because it makes men mean.

Geneva: Why does Uncle Sam wear red, white, and blue suspenders?
Guthrie: I have no idea.
Geneva: To hold up his pants.

Geneva: What has spots, weighs four tons, and loves peanuts?

Guthrie: I don't know.
Geneva: An elephant with the measles.

Geneva: What does a worm do in a
cornfield?
Guthrie: I have no idea.
Geneva: It goes in one ear and out the
other.

Geneva: What animal is satisfied with the
least nourishment?
Guthrie: You tell me.
Geneva: Moths. They eat nothing but
holes.

Geneva: What do you call a carrot who
insults a farmer?
Guthrie: I give up.
Geneva: A fresh vegetable.

Geneva: What has one eye, one horn, and
flies?
Guthrie: Who knows?
Geneva: A half-blind rhinoceros in an
airplane.

Geneva: What do you get if you cross a
hummingbird with a bell?
Guthrie: You've got me.
Geneva: A humdinger.

⚭

Geneva: What does Jack's giant do when
he plays football?
Guthrie: My mind is a blank.
Geneva: He fee-fi-fo-fumbles.

⚭

Geneva: What man slept in his clothes for
100 years?
Guthrie: That's a mystery.
Geneva: Rip Van Wrinkled.

⚭

Geneva: What do whales do when they
feel sad?
Guthrie: Tell me.
Geneva: Blubber.

⚭

Geneva: What kind of soda can't you
drink?
Guthrie: I don't have the foggiest.
Geneva: Baking soda.

⚭

Geneva: What kind of toys does a
psychiatrist's child play with?
Guthrie: It's unknown to me.
Geneva: Mental blocks.

Geneva: What two garden vegetables fight
crime?
Guthrie: I'm in the dark.
Geneva: Beetman and Radish.

Geneva: What kind of ties can't you wear?
Guthrie: Search me.
Geneva: Railroad ties.

10

Gustave & Gilberta Goofy

Gustave: Who's white, has two eyes made out of coal, and can't move fast?
Gilberta: Beats me.
Gustave: Frosty the Slowman.

Gustave: Why is it bad to write a letter on an empty stomach?
Gilberta: I can't guess.
Gustave: Because it's much better to write on paper.

Gustave: Why was the 2,000-year-old flower wrapped in strips of cloth?
Gilberta: I have no idea.
Gustave: It was a chrysanthemummy.

Gustave: What is the best thing to put in
a pie?
Gilberta: I don't know.
Gustave: Your teeth.

⁂

Gustave: What belongs to you, but is used
more often by others?
Gilberta: I have no idea.
Gustave: Your name.

⁂

Gustave: What do you do if you smash
your toe?
Gilberta: You tell me.
Gustave: You call a toe truck.

⁂

Gustave: What changes color every two
seconds?
Gilberta: I give up.
Gustave: A chameleon with the hiccups.

⁂

Gustave: What happens when an ear of
corn gets dandruff?
Gilberta: Who knows?
Gustave: It ends up with cornflakes.

⁂

Gustave: What does the sneezing champion of the Olympics win?
Gilberta: You've got me.
Gustave: A cold medal.

Gustave: What is worse than being with a fool?
Gilberta: My mind is a blank.
Gustave: Fooling with a bee.

Gustave: What kind of bee drops its honey?
Gilberta: That's a mystery.
Gustave: A spilling bee.

Gustave: What's the difference between a barber and a woman with many children?
Gilberta: Tell me.
Gustave: One has razors to shave, the other has shavers to raise.

Gustave: What squawks and jumps out of airplanes?
Gilberta: I don't have the foggiest.
Gustave: A parrot-trooper.

Gustave: What do attorneys wear to
work?
Gilberta: It's unknown to me.
Gustave: Lawsuits.

11

Goofy Definitions

Amount: What a soldier in the cavalry rides.

Antiques: Merchandise sold for old times' sake.

Appeal: What a banana comes in.

Beatnik: What Nick's father does when Nick is naughty.

Boycott: A bed for a small male child.

Beastly Weather: Raining cats and dogs.

Carpet: A dog or cat who enjoys riding in an automobile.

Circle: A round straight line with a hole in the middle.

Compliment: The applause that refreshes.

Endangered Species: A kid who gets straight Fs on his report card.

Falsehood: Someone who pretends to be a gangster.

Fodder: The man who married Mudder.

Gruesome: A little taller than before.

Half-wit: A person who spends half his time thinking up wisecracks and definitions.

Knapsack: A sleeping bag.

 ⋘⋙

Map: Something that will tell you everything except how to fold it up again.

 ⋘⋙

Pedestrian: A father who has kids who can drive.

 ⋘⋙

Stork: The bird with the big bill.

 ⋘⋙

Screen door: What kids get a bang out of.

 ⋘⋙

Turtle: A reptile who lives in a mobile home.

 ⋘⋙

Ventriloquist: A person who talks to himself for a living.

12

Goofy Doctors

Patient: You're charging me ten dollars and all you did was paint my throat?
Doctor: What did you expect for ten dollars—wallpaper? Next.

Patient: Don't you think I should get a second opinion?
Doctor: Sure. Come back tomorrow.

Patient: What would you take for this cold?
Doctor: Make me an offer.

Patient: Am I going to die?
Doctor: That's the last thing you're going to do.

Wife: Thank you so much for making this house call to see my husband.

Doctor: Think nothing of it. There is another man sick in the neighborhood, and I thought I could kill two birds with one stone.

Patient: Am I getting better?

Doctor: I don't know—let me feel your purse.

Patient: Should I file my nails?

Doctor: No. Throw them away like everybody else.

Patient: Doctor, my child just swallowed a pen. What should I do?

Doctor: Use a pencil.

Patient: Doctor, you've gotta do something for me. I snore so loudly that I wake myself up.

Doctor: In that case, sleep in another room.

Patient: Doctor, what's the difference between an itch and an allergy?
Doctor: About $35.

Patient: Doctor, nobody can figure out what's wrong with me. I've got the oddest collection of symptoms.
Doctor: Have you had it before?
Patient: Yes.
Doctor: Well, you've got it again.

Patient: Doctor, what am I really allergic to?
Doctor: Paying my bills.

Nurse: Doctor, I just wanted to let you know that there is an invisible man in your waiting room.
Doctor: Tell him I can't see him now.

Patient: Doctor, my child just swallowed a dozen aspirins. What should I do?
Doctor: Give him a headache.

Patient: Doctor, there's something wrong with my stomach.

Goofy doctor: Keep your coat buttoned and nobody will notice it.

Patient: Doctor, is it a boy?
Doctor: Well, the one in the middle is.

Doctor: I've never seen anything quite like these second-degree burns on both your ears. How did you get them?
Goofy Gretta: Well, the phone rang and I picked up the steam iron by mistake.
Doctor: But what about the other ear?
Goofy Gretta: They called back.

Patient: Doctor, I think everyone tries to take advantage of me.
Goofy psychiatrist: That's silly. It's a perfectly normal feeling.
Patient: Is it really? Thanks for your help, Doctor. How much do I owe you?
Goofy psychiatrist: How much do you have?

Patient: How can I avoid falling hair?
Doctor: Step to one side.

Nurse: There's a man outside with a
    wooden leg named Smith.
Doctor: What's the name of his other leg?

Patient: What should I do if my
    temperature goes up another point?
Doctor: Sell!

Patient: How long will I live?
Doctor: You should live to be 80.
Patient: I am 80.
Doctor: What did I tell you?

Patient: My hair is coming out. What can
    you give me to keep it in?
Doctor: A cigar box.

13
Goofy Knock-Knocks

Knock, knock.
Who's there?
Osborn.
Osborn who?
Osborn in August.

Knock, knock.
Who's there?
Max.
Max who?
Max no difference. Let me in.

Knock, knock.
Who's there?
Kleenex.
Kleenex who?
Kleenex are prettier than dirty necks.

Knock, knock.
Who's there?
Hewlett.
Hewlett who?
Hewlett the cat out of the bag?

Knock, knock.
Who's there?
Adore.
Adore who?
Adore is between us. Open up.

Knock, knock.
Who's there?
Eyewash.
Eyewash who?
Eyewash I had a million dollars.

Knock, knock.
Who's there?
Stan.
Stan who?
Stan back! I'm coming in.

Knock, knock.
Who's there?
Alison.
Alison who?
Alison Wonderland.

Knock, knock.
Who's there?
Dewey.
Dewey who?
Dewey have to listen to all this knocking?

Knock, knock.
Who's there?
Wooden.
Wooden who?
Wooden you like to go out with me?

Knock, knock.
Who's there?
Adele.
Adele who?
Adele is where the farmer's in.

Knock, knock.
Who's there?
Ether.
Ether who?
Ether bunny.

Knock, knock.
Who's there?

Caesar.
Caesar who?
Caesar jolly good fellow, Caesar jolly good
  fellow.

Knock, knock.
Who's there?
Consumption.
Consumption who?
Consumption be done about these jokes?

Knock, knock.
Who's there?
Thatcher.
Thatcher who?
Thatcher was a funny joke.

Knock, knock.
Who's there?
Boo-hoo.
Boo-hoo who?
Boo-hoo-hoo.
Boo-hoo-hoo who?
Boo-hoo-hoo-hoo.
Boo-hoo-hoo-hoo who?
Boo-hoo-hoo-hoo-hoo.
Boo-hoo-hoo-hoo-hoo who?
Stop it! You're breaking my heart.

Knock, knock.
Who's there?
Jupiter.
Jupiter who?
Jupiter fly in my soup?

Knock, knock.
Who's there?
Amaryllis.
Amaryllis who?
Amaryllis state agent—wanna buy
    a house?

14

Goofy Students

First student: The teacher gave me an F-.
Second student: Why did she do that?
First student: She says I didn't learn anything this year, and I've probably forgotten most of the stuff I learned last year!

Teacher: Mrs. Grey, your son is a constant troublemaker. How do you put up with him?
Mrs. Grey: I can't. That's why I send him to school.

Teacher: What, besides a supersonic jet, goes faster than the speed of sound?
Student: My Aunt Gladys when she talks.

Teacher: When was the great depression?

Student: Last week when I got my report card.

Teacher: What's a leading cause of dry skin?
Student: Towels.

Teacher: Can you name two responsibilities you have at home?
Student: Get out and stay out.

Teacher: Name two cities in Kentucky.
Student: Okay. I'll name one George and the other Gene.

Goofy student: Teacher, is there life after death?
Teacher: Why do you ask?
Goofy student: I may need the extra time to finish all this homework you gave us.

Teacher: Gene, what's the first thing you should do with a barrel of crude oil?
Goofy Gene: Teach it some manners.

Teacher: Everyone knows we should conserve energy. Greg, name one way we can do that.

Goofy Greg: By staying in bed all day.

Teacher: Gabriel, how many books did you finish over the summer?

Goofy Gabriel: None. My brother stole my box of crayons.

Teacher: When did George Washington die?

Goofy Grant: It was just a few days before they buried him.

Teacher: Why should we never use the word "ain't"?

Goofy George: Because it ain't correct.

15
Going Goofy

Stuffy singer: I sing with the voice of a
bird.
Listener: I know—a crow.

Comedian: I never tell jokes about ceilings
because the punch lines always go over
everyone's head.

If you order bison steaks at a restaurant,
what does the waiter bring you after
the meal?
A Buffalo Bill.

Jerad: Did you hear about the wall that
turned to a life of crime?
Jackie: No. What did he do?
Jerad: He went around holding up ceilings.

Two fine and devout Irish ladies end up in heaven:

"Isn't this grand, Gracie? Every night we go to bingo, there's a lot of singing and dancing, and they have all the old Alan Ladd movies."

"Yes, indeed, Gertrude, and you know if it weren't for that silly oat bran, we'd have been here ten years earlier."

If, in a restaurant, you must choose between eating an elephant egg or a 500-pound canary egg, which should you choose?

A 500-pound canary egg, because everyone hates elephant yolks.

"That's a beautiful stuffed tiger you've got there. Where did you get him?"

"In India when I was on a hunting expedition with my uncle."

"What's he stuffed with?"

"My uncle."

First Kid: Did you know that Daniel Boone's brothers were all famous doctors?

Second Kid: No way.

First kid: Don't tell me you never heard of
the Boone Docs?

I'm not as stupid as I look. Last week a
wiseguy tried to sell me the Statue of
Liberty and I didn't give him any
money—until he gave me a ten-year
guarantee on the flame.

People are always criticizing my looks.
After I took out my last blind date,
she went home and reported having a
close encounter of the third kind.

Have you heard of Amoeba State Prison?
It's so small it only has one cell.

My father taught me to swim when I was
five years old. He took me down to
the river and threw me in. I wouldn't
have minded, but people were ice
skating at the time.

I don't think my parents like me. When I
was a kid, they had me memorize a
phony address just in case I got lost.

Scientist: Do you know what will happen
when man pollutes outer space?
Man: Yeah. The Milky Way will curdle.

Everybody in school thought I'd grow up
to be a famous comedian. They voted
me the person most likely to be
laughed at.

I just heard that Italy is sponsoring a new
award for excellence in the field of
junk food. It's called the Nobel Pizza
Prize.

Yesterday a beautiful girl told me I
reminded her of her favorite boxer.
And his name was Fido.

I think our currency is headed for another
fall on the world market. Yesterday, I
looked at a five-dollar bill and
Abraham Lincoln was wearing a crash
helmet.

Man: I got airsick again last week.
Woman: Oh, were you in an airplane?
Man: No. In Los Angeles.

As a child, every time I went to a party they'd make me play pin-the-tail-on-the donkey. Afterwards, I couldn't sit for a week.

In a bakery window: *Pie Like Mother Used to Buy.*

Two frogs were sitting on a lily pad. One leaned over to the other and said, "Time sure is fun when you're having flies."

First kid: Hey, I have an idea!
Second Kid: Beginner's luck.

16

Goofy Goodies

You can't convince me crime doesn't pay. Last week I was standing on a curb and a limousine pulled up in front of me. A chauffeur got out, rolled out a red carpet, and opened the back door for a mugger who robbed me.

In a Maine classroom, Miss Hubbard was telling her pupils how people from different states were given nicknames that designated something of significance about their state.

"For example," she explained, "people from North Carolina are called 'Tar Heels,' people from Ohio are called 'Buck eyes,' and those from Indiana are called 'Hoosiers.'

"Can any of you tell me what they call people from our state of Maine?"

Arlene raised her hand, "Maniacs!"

Garth: I'm going to have to let that new
    secretary go.
Gertha: Don't you think he's learning
    word processing fast enough?
Garth: I don't think so. There's too much
    White-Out on the computer screen!

The trouble with dark horse candidates is
    you can't find out about their track
    record until you're saddled with them.

Talk about being dumb. A robber jumped
    out of an alley, pointed a gun at a man
    and said, "Give me 50 dollars."
The victim replied, "I'm sorry I don't have
    50 dollars. Can you break a
    hundred-dollar bill?"

"My cat ate a whole ball of wool."
"So what?"
"So her kittens were all born wearing
    sweaters."
"That's some yarn."
"Well, I'm a knit-wit."

If dentists pull police officers' teeth out,
what do police officers do to dentists'
teeth?
Pull them over.

I live in a high-crime neighborhood—even
our police station has a burglar alarm.

If a gardener has a green thumb, who has
a purple thumb?
A near-sighted carpenter.

Bachelor: Listen, baby, you've got to admit
that guys like me don't grow on trees.
Girl: No, they swing from them!

Buyer: Hey, you told me you had purebred
police dogs for sale. This animal is the
mangiest, dirtiest, scrawniest mutt I've
ever laid eyes on! How can you get
away with calling him a police dog?
Breeder: He works undercover.

Greg: How was your trip to Helsinki?
Gene: Terrible! All our luggage vanished
into Finn air!

Lady: What a cute little boy. What's your
  name, sweetheart?
Little boy: Connor.
Lady: Can you tell me your full name?
Little boy: Connor Stop That!

Gwin: Well, excuse me for living!
Gilbert: Okay, but don't let it happen
  again.

His teeth are so yellow, every time he
  smiles in traffic all the cars slow down
  to see whether they should stop or go.

First man (reading statistics): Do you
  know that every time I breathe,
  someone dies?
Second man: Have you tried mouthwash?

"My business is down in the dumps," said
  the garbage man.

Five-year-old Bobby sat on the front
  porch holding his cat. A little girl who

lived around the corner approached him and said, "What's your cat's name?"

"Ben Hur," replied the little boy.

"How did you happen to call it that?"

"We used to call it Ben—until it had kittens."

17

Genuinely Goofy

What steps should you take if a tiger
  charges you?
Long ones.

What did the judge say when the skunk
  came into the courtroom?
Odor in the court!

When is a black dog not a black dog?
When he is a greyhound.

What is the difference between a hungry
  person and a greedy person?
One longs to eat and the other eats too long.

What is smaller than an ant's mouth?
An ant's dinner.

What is the surest way to double your money?
Fold it.

What kind of clothes do Supreme Court judges wear?
Lawsuits.

Why is a sleeping baby like a hijacking?
Because it's a kid napping.

Do you know why the cow jumped over the moon?
The farmer had cold hands.

How can you tell there's an elephant under your bed?
The ceiling is very close.

What is a diploma?
Da man who fixa da pipes when dey leak.

I have eyes, but I can't see. What am I?
A potato.

What's the difference between kissing
   your sister and kissing your
   sweetheart?
About 25 seconds.

How do you stop a charging lion?
Take away his credit cards.

Where do cows go when they want a
   night out?
To the moo-vies!

What is the difference between a tuna
   fish and a piano?
You can't tune a fish.

What is deaf, dumb, and blind and
   always tells the truth?
A mirror.

18

Good-Humored Goofies

Where can you always find happiness?
In the dictionary.

How do you make a slow employee fast?
Don't give him anything to eat for a while.

What is worse than a centipede with
    corns?
A hippopotamus with chapped lips.

What adds color and flavor to a very
    popular old pastime?
Lipstick.

Why did the comedian's wife sue for
    divorce?
She claimed he was trying to joke her to death.

What is the center of gravity?
V.

What do you call a nut that never
remembers?
A forget-me-nut.

What did the nearsighted Gingerbread
Boy use for eyes?
Contact raisins.

What kind of lights did Noah have on
the ark?
Floodlights.

What animal drops from the clouds?
The rain, dear.

Why should you borrow money from a
pessimist?
Because he never expects to get it back.

If you threw a green shoe into the Red
    Sea, what would it become?
Wet.

What is the saddest bird alive?
The bluebird.

How many hamburgers can you eat on an
    empty stomach?
*Only one. After that your stomach is no longer
    empty.*

What can you make by putting two
    banana peels together?
A pair of slippers.

19

Gadzooks! More Goofies

Greta: I always get sick the night before I take a trip.
Greg: Then why don't you leave a day earlier?

First boy: A train just passed.
Second boy: How can you tell?
First boy: I can see its tracks.

Gene: Did you hear about the guy from Rome who wanted to swim the English Channel, but couldn't?
Geanie: No, what about him?
Gene: He could only swim in Italian.

Gretchen: An apple a day keeps the doctor away.
Gabe: What keeps friends away?

Gretchen: Bad breath.

✐

Mr. Green: Why, when I first came to this city, I was jobless, penniless, shoeless, and without a shred of clothing!
Interviewer: You mean . . .
Mr. Green: That's right! I was born here!

✐

Georgeina: Did you hear about the terrible accident? A pink cruise ship collided with a purple cruise ship.
George: What happened?
Georgeina: All the passengers were marooned!

✐

Gwen: So, you're expecting your seventh child! What do you think you'll call it?
Gina: I think I'll call it Quits!

✐

My husband has a one-track mind—and it's the slow lane.

✐

Customer: Are 500-pound canaries intelligent?

Shopkeeper: Of course not, they're all
    bird-brained.

Crooks are bolder than ever. The last time
    I was robbed, the mugger gave me his
    card in case I was ever in the
    neighborhood again.

Ranch Visitor: This is the biggest ranch
    I've ever seen. How many head of
    cattle have you got over there?
Rancher: I can't tell. They're facing the
    wrong way.

Rumor has it that a boxer who gets beat
    up in a fight is usually a sore loser.

Crime can be really bad in the East in the
    wintertime. During the last blizzard, a
    bunch of kids made a snowman. Five
    minutes after it was finished, a crook
    came along and mugged it.

A little boy showed his teacher his
    drawing, entitled "America the
    Beautiful." In the center was an

airplane covered with apples, pears, oranges, and bananas.

"What is this?" the teacherr asked, pointing to the airplane.

"That," answered the boy, "is the fruited plane."

Last week my son in college had a very painful amputation.
I cut off his allowance.

Griff: My Uncle Guy is running for mayor.
Gretta: Honest?
Griff: No, but that's not stopping him.

We had food fight in the school cafeteria today. The food won.

Guy: Every morning I dream I'm falling from a 10-story building and just before I hit the ground, I wake up.
Grace: That's terrible. What are you going to do about it?
Guy: I'm going to move into a 15-story building. I need more sleep.

Geoffe: Did you know there was a
    kidnapping down the street?
Geaney: No, what happened?
Geoffe: His mother woke him up.

Gerald: What's flat at the bottom, pointed
    at the top, and has ears?
Gene: I give up.
Gerald: A mountain.
Gene: Oh yeah, what about the ears?
Gerald: Haven't you ever heard of
    mountaineers?

The doctor calls with the results of Griff's
    physical.
"Griff, I've got bad news and worse news.
    The bad news is that you have 24
    hours to live."
"Oh, no," says Griff, "that's rotten, but
    what could be worse than that?"
"I've been trying to get you since
    yesterday."

A man suffering from terrible headaches
    goes to his doctor.
"Your brain is diseased and something
    must be done," says the doctor.
"What can be done?"

"The only possibility is a new brain
transplant technique, but the problem
is that the cost of a brain is not
covered by medical insurance."

"Doc, I've got some money; what'll it cost
me?"

"Depends on the donor," says the doctor.
"A secretary's brain will cost you about
$35,000 and salesmen's brains cost
closer to $150,000. On the other
hand, an executive's brain will set you
back close to a quarter of a million
dollars."

"Wait a second!" says the patient, "The
difference between $35,000 and
$250,000 is vast. How can you justify
such an incredible discrepency?"

"Simple! The executive's brain has hardly
been used."

Old baseball players never have mental
breakdowns. They just go a little batty.

How about the story about the snake
trainers? It was rather charming.

Watching his new employee count out
the day's receipts, the boss walked

over and asked the man where he got
  his financial training.
"Yale," he answers.
"Good. And what is your name?"
"Yackson."

The gate between heaven and hell broke,
  and St. Peter called to the devil, "It's
  your turn to fix it."
"Sorry," the devil said. "We are too busy
  fixing our heating system to worry
  about a little thing like a gate."
"If you don't fix it," said St. Peter, "I'll
  have to sue you for breaking our
  working agreement."
"Is that so?" the devil asked. "Where are
  you going to find a lawyer?"

The meat was so tough at lunch today,
  half the class was kept after school
  so we could finish chewing it.

20
Goofy Gags

What did one tail pipe say to the other
tail pipe?
I'm exhausted.

Why does electricity shock people?
Because it doesn't know how to conduct itself.

Who can stay single even if he marries
many women?
A minister.

What has a heart in its head?
Lettuce.

If you were dying and had only a dime,
what would you buy?
A pack of lifesavers.

What do you call a midget novelist?
A short story writer.

Why does a fireman wear red suspenders?
To hold up his pants.

When is it proper to refer to a person as a
pig?
When he is a boar.

How do you make a Big Mac monster
burger?
You put two people patties, special sauce,
lettuce, cheese, pickles, and onions on
a sesame seed bun.

What animal doesn't play fair?
The cheetah.

What's the best way to paint a rabbit?
With hare spray.

What will stay hot longest in the
refrigerator?
Red peppers.

What word do most people like best?
The last.

Why did the traffic light turn red?
*If you had to change in front of all those
people, you'd turn red too.*

What happens when a chimp twists his
ankle?
He gets a monkey wrench.

What pen is never used for writing?
A pigpen.

21

Galloping Goofies

What is it that even the smartest person
will always overlook?
His nose.

What keeps the moon from falling?
Its beams, of course.

What kind of robbery may not be
dangerous?
A safe robbery.

What does the plumber say to his wife
when she talks too much?
Pipe down.

What kind of fish is the most stupid?
A simple salmon.

If you were locked in a cemetery at night,
how would you get out?
Use a skeleton key.

What kind of song do you sing in a car?
A cartoon.

When can you see yourself in a place
you've never been?
When you look into a mirror.

What does a garden say when it laughs?
Hoe, hoe, hoe.

What is the last thing you take off before
going to bed?
Your feet from the floor.

Why do birds fly south for the winter?
Because it's too far to walk.

What do you call someone whose opinion
differs from your own?
A radical.

When is it right for you to lie?
When you are in bed.

How do sailors identify Long Island?
By the sound.

How can a leopard change his spots?
By moving.

Who is Ferris?
He's a big wheel at the amusement park.

Why does a person who is sick lose his sense of touch?
Because he doesn't feel well.

22

Goofies Galore

Which burns longer—a white candle or a
    black candle?
Neither. Both burn shorter.

If you were invited out to dinner and,
    after sitting down, you saw nothing
    but a beet, what would you say?
"That beet's all!"

Which key is the hardest to turn?
A donkey.

In what month do girls talk the least?
February—because it's the shortest.

Which bird can lift the heaviest weight?
The crane.

Who was the world's greatest glutton?
A man who bolted a door, threw up a window, and then sat down and swallowed a whole story.

How would you define the daffodil?
A goofy pickle.

What do they call a towel that you look at but never use?
A guest towel.

What two flowers grow best in a zoo?
Dandelions and tiger lilies.

When is an elevator not an elevator?
When it's going down.

If your dog were eating your book, what would you do?
I would take the words right out of his mouth.

Why are telephone rates so high in Iran?
Because everyone speaks Persian-to-Persian.

What cord is full of knots which no one
can untie?
A cord of wood.

When do hens change their sex?
At night—when they become roosters.

When the clock strikes 13, what time is
it?
Time to get the clock fixed.

Why is a kiss like gossip?
Because it goes from mouth to mouth.

What do they call a butcher's dance?
A meatball.

It takes 12 one-cent stamps to make a
dozen. How many six-cent stamps
does it take to make a dozen?
*It takes 12 of anything to make a dozen—even
six-cent stamps.*

23

Giggling Goofies

If you see the handwriting on the wall,
    there's a child in the family.

I come from a broken home. My kids have
    broken everything in it.

The food in our school cafeteria is so bad
    that last night they caught a mouse
    trying to phone out for pizza.

We have a kid in class who dresses like a
    million bucks.
Everything he wears is all wrinkled and
    green.

Popeye who?
Popeye've got to have the car tonight.

Is that your head, or did someone plant a
   pumpkin on your neck?

"For the last ten years my mother-in-law
   has been living with my wife and me
   in the same apartment."
"So, why don't you tell her to get out?"
"I can't. It's her apartment."

There's too much violence on television
   these days. I watched TV the other
   day and saw two murders, six fights,
   an earthquake, and a nuclear disaster.
   That's the last time I'll get up to watch
   Saturday morning cartoons.

Gina: My dog has a sweet tooth.
Gabe: How do you know that?
Gina: He only chases bakery trucks.

Let a smile be your umbrella and you'll
   end up with a mouthful of rain.

Gerald: I'm giving my girl a striking and
   timely present for her birthday.
Garth: What did you get her?

Gerald: An alarm clock.

Once I ate in a restaurant that was so bad I got food poisoning just from opening the menu.

Life on other planets must be intelligent. They've had enough sense not to establish diplomatic relations with earth so far.

Gloria: Did you hear about the head of cabbage, the hose, and the bottle of ketchup that were having a race?
Gretta: No, how did it go?
Gloria: The cabbage was a head, the hose was still running, and the bottle of sauce was trying to catch up.

Are those ears really yours or are you wearing pierced ear muffs?

If your shoes were two sizes larger, you'd be Big Foot's twin.

They call him King Chicken because he's
the biggest cluck in town.

What is a nasty bug that eats up a poor
farmer's cotton?
An evil weevil.

You tell 'em, banana, you've been skinned.

You tell 'em, aviator, you're a high flyer.

You tell 'em, operator, you've got their
number.

24

Goony Goofies

What kind of waiter never accepts tips?
A dumbwaiter.

What is the difference between a cat and
a match?
*The cat lights on its feet and the match on its
head.*

What happens when the human body is
completely submerged in water?
The telephone rings.

How many Californians does it take to
replace a lightbulb?
*One to change the bulb and two to share the
experience.*

What can't you hold for five minutes yet
    it's as light as a feather?
Your breath.

What headlines do women like least?
Wrinkles.

Why can't the world ever come to an end?
Because it's round.

How can you tell if a student is hungry?
When he devours books.

How do you play Russian roulette in
    India?
*You play the flute with six cobras around
    you—and one of them is deaf.*

Is Ballpoint really the name of your pig?
No—that's just his pen name.

Who was the greatest Irish inventor?
Pat Pending.

What happened when two geese had a
head-on collision?
They got goose bumps.

What do you call a 30-pound book you
use as a weapon?
A book club.

How does your stamp album feel when
it's kept in the refrigerator?
Cool, calm, and collected.

Which is faster—hot or cold?
Hot's faster. You can catch cold.

Where do they send homeless dogs?
To an arfanage.

25
Great Goofies

How did the rocket lose his job?
He was fired.

Why did the boy take a hammer to bed
  with him?
He wanted to hit the sack.

Where is the best place to have a broken
  bone?
On someone else.

What is worse than raining cats and dogs?
Hailing taxis and buses.

What did Paul Revere say when he
  finished his famous ride?
Whoa!

Why does a dog wag its tail?
Because it wants to.

What did the grape say when it was
    stepped on by an elephant?
Nothing . . . it just gave a little whine.

What should you do when your sister
    falls asleep in church?
Polka.

Where is the capital of the United
    States?
All over the world.

What is always coming but never arrives?
Tomorrow.

How do you spell Mississippi with one
    eye?
Close one eye and spell it.

What do you get when a bird flies into a
    fan?
Shredded tweet.

Which is correct: The yolk of an egg is
    white? Or the yolks of eggs are white?
Neither, the yolk of an egg is yellow.

What would a home be without children?
Quiet.

Why did the farmer put the cow on the
    scale?
He wanted to see how much the milky weighed.

26

Golden Goofies

Who was the first man to make a monkey
   of himself?
Darwin.

What are the largest ants in the world?
Elephants.

What do they call someone who can stick
   to a diet?
A good loser.

How far is it from one end of the earth to
   the other?
*A day's journey (24 hours—the earth's
   rotation).*

What did the Gingerbread Boy find on
his bed?
A cookie sheet, of course!

What is the best thing about tiny TV
sets?
Tiny commercials.

Why do we go to bed?
Because the bed will not come to us.

What increases in value by half when you
turn it upside down?
The number 6.

What time is it when an elephant sits on
your fence?
Time to buy a new fence.

When does a boat show affection?
When it hugs the shore.

What does 36 inches make in Glasgow?
One Scotland Yard.

Why can't it rain for two days
    continually?
Because there is always a night in between.

Why is a bank robbery like a pair of
    suspenders?
Because they are both holdups.

What is the best way to make time go by
    fast?
Use the spur of the moment.

What kinds of animals can jump higher
    than the Statue of Liberty?
Any kind. The Statue of Liberty can't jump.

Why do we dress little girl babies in pink
    and boy babies in blue?
Because they can't dress themselves.

27

Giddy Goofies

I got straight F's in the sixth grade. That's not good—but it's a slight improvement over what I did in sixth grade last year.

I had one friend who was a real dummy. He lost his shoes one time because he put them on the wrong feet. Then he couldn't remember whose feet he put them on.

When do Eskimos travel in heavy traffic?
At mush hour.

What do you have when you extend your little finger?
A Goofy handkerchief.

When does a horse talk?
Whinny wants to.

Why do goofy people have cabbage and
 Arabs have oil?
The goofy people had first choice.

How do you spell pickle backwards?
P-I-C-K-L-E B-A-C-K-W-A-R-D-S.

Where does bacteria go on vacation?
Germany.

Then there was a goofy man who put
on one boot because the weather forecaster
called for only one foot of snow.

How do you spell blind pig in six letters?
B-L-N-D P-G.

Where do you buy laundry detergent?
In a soapermarket.

Her luck was so bad that her contacts got cataracts.

How do army frogs march?
Hop, 2, 3, 4!

28

Grand Goofies

How does an elephant get in a tree?
*He hides in an acorn and waits for a squirrel
to carry him up.*

Where do you find tigers?
Depends on where you leave them.

Who hit the bulls-eye eight times?
500 goofy sharpshooters.

How do you make antifreeze?
Hide her nightie.

What is gross stupidity?
144 goofy people.

Where do dead letters go?
To the ghost office.

He was so slow they had to show him how the wastebasket worked the first day on his new job.

How does an artist break up with his girlfriend?
He gives her the brush-off.

Where's the best place to find books about trees?
A branch library.

Two goofy men were building a house. One, examining each nail as he picked it up, was tossing about half of them away.
"What's the matter?" asked the second goofy man.
"Half of these nails have the head on the wrong end."
"You fool, those are for the other side of the house!"

How did the jewel thief wake up every
    morning?
To a burglar alarm.

When the May Day parade was still a
big deal in Moscow, a Westerner noted a
phalanx of goofy Soviet economists
marching between military units.

"Why are the goofy economists
marching in ranks with the army?" the
Westerner asked a bystander.

"You'd be surprised at the damage they
do," he replied.

Where can you find the finest basements?
On the best-cellar list.

First goofy man: I just got a bicycle for my
    girlfriend.
Second goofy man: How did you get such
    a good trade?

How did the barber get rid of his
    unwanted rabbits?
He used hare remover.

29

Goofy Gallery

What would happen if all the goofy
people in Chicago jumped into Lake
Michigan?
*Lake Michigan would end up with a ring
around it.*

Did you hear about the four goofy
people in a pickup truck that drove into a
canal? The two in the front were saved,
but the two in back were lost because the
tailgate was stuck.

How do you mail a boat?
You ship it.

One kid in our class dresses terribly.
The only things that match are his belt
size and his IQ.

Man: How many slopes did they have at
  the ski resort you went to?
Woman: Three . . . beginners, intermediate,
  and call-an-ambulance!

Where do fish go to get a degree?
To tunaversities.

There was this goofy man who tried to
  have his marriage annulled when he
  found out her father had no license for
  the gun.

How do you catch an electric eel?
With a lightning rod.

When my little girl got married, I
didn't lose a daughter, I gained a son. He
moved in with us.

When you fill me up, I still look empty.
  What am I?
A balloon.

Did you hear about the goofy man who willed his body to science? Science is contesting the will.

How many goofy people does it take to eat a rabbit dinner?

Three. One to feast, and two to watch in each direction for cars.

30
A Gunnysack Full of Goofies

If tires hold up cars, what holds up an
airplane?
Hijackers!

❧

What state is like a father?
Pa.

❧

What state was important to Noah?
Ark.

❧

What state is like a piece of clothing?
New Jersey.

❧

What do you get if you drop limburger
cheese in the toaster?

You get out of the kitchen as fast as you can.

What's a cat's favorite side dish at lunch?
Micearoni and cheese.

What's black, covered with feathers, and
weighs 2,000 pounds?
An elephant that's been tarred and feathered.

What is gray and stamps out jungle fires?
Smokey the Elephant.

What is the worst flower to invite to a
party?
A daffodull.

What's the difference between Christopher
Columbus and the lid of a dish?
One is a discoverer, the other is a dish coverer.

What do you get when you cross an owl
with an oyster?
An animal that drops pearls of wisdom.

What mouse heads the House of
Representatives?
The Squeaker of the House.

What U.S. president got hit by a truck?
George Squashington.

What do you need to spot an iceberg 20
miles away?
Good ice sight.

What would you get if you crossed an
alligator with a pickle?
A crocodill.

What occurs once in a minute, twice in a
moment, but not once in a hundred
years?
The letter m.

What do you call two convicts who
become buddies in jail?
Pen pals.

What is the difference between an
    11-year-old girl and a 15-year-old girl?
A 5-dollar difference in your phone bill.

What did Adam say on the day before
    Christmas?
It's Christmas, Eve.

What is the difference between a lollipop
    and a chicken?
One you suck and one you pluck.

What do you give an elk with
    indigestion?
Elk-a-Seltzer.

What should you do if you find yourself
    with water on the knee, water on the
    elbow, and water on the brain?
Turn off the shower.

What happens when the sun gets tired?
It sets a while.

What kind of teeth can you buy for a
dollar?
Buck teeth.

What ice cream do monkeys eat?
Chocolate chimp.

31
Glorious Goofies

What is harder than cutting school?
Gluing it back together.

What happens when frogs get married?
They live hoppily ever after.

What is the skunk's motto?
Walk softly and carry a big stink.

What is a rabbit's favorite song?
Hoppy Birthday.

What kind of ducks rob banks?
Safequackers.

What is purple and crazy?

A grape nut.

⚬∞⚬

What kind of stroller do you wheel an
    infant insect in?
A baby buggy.

⚬∞⚬

What do you get when you chop down a
    tuna tree?
Fish sticks.

⚬∞⚬

What is pronounced like one letter,
    written with three letters, and belongs
    to all animals?
Eye.

⚬∞⚬

What is the wife of a jeweler called?
Ruby.

⚬∞⚬

What does a tiger do when it rains?
It gets wet.

⚬∞⚬

What is the difference between a
    chocolate chip cookie and an
    elephant?
You can't dunk an elephant in your milk.

What did the prisoner say when he
    bumped into the governor?
Pardon me!

What is beautiful, gray, and wears glass
    slippers?
Cinderelephant.

What is black and white and hides in
    caves?
A zebra who owes money.

What city is named after a small stone?
Little Rock, Arkansas.

What is orange, runs on batteries, and
    costs six million dollars?
The Bionic Carrot.

What do Alexander the Great and
    Smokey the Bear have in common?
They both have the same middle name.

What rolls in the mud and plays
trick-or-treat?
The Halloween Pig.

❦

What has seeds, a stem, and swings from
tree to tree?
Tarzan and the grapes.

❦

What is large and gray and bumps into
submarines?
A near-sighted hippo scuba diver.

❦

What does a slice of toast wear to bed?
Jam-mies.

❦

What cheese can't stop talking?
Chatter cheese.

❦

What piece of furniture will never learn
to swim?
The sink.

❦

What is the snootiest dog?
A cocky spaniel.

32
Galleria of Goofies

What do plumbers smoke?
Pipes.

What do you get if you light a duck's
   tail?
A firequacker.

What do you have when 134 strawberries
   try to get through the same door?
A strawberry jam.

What do you get if you cross a dentist
   with the tooth fairy?
A mouth full of quarters.

What do you call mail sent to a cat?
Kitty letter.

What's gray and spins around and
    around?
A hippo stuck in a revolving door.

What do you call an elephant hitchhiker?
A 2¹/₂-ton pickup.

What do you get if you cross a rhinoceros
    and a goose?
An animal that honks before it runs you over.

What did the rabbits do when they got
    married?
Went on their bunnymoon.

What invention allows people to walk
    through walls?
Doors.

What do you call 500 Indians without
    any apples?
The Indian apple-less 500.

What does a tuba call his father?
Ooom-papa.

What's the difference between a jeweler
and a jailer?
One sells watches, while the other watches cells.

What do you call an ice cream man in the
state of Arizona?
A Good Yuma man.

What has a foot at each end and a foot in
the middle?
A yardstick.

What kind of dress do you have, but
never wear?
Your address.

What do diets and promises have in
common?
They are always being broken.

What should you do if you accidently eat
some microfilm?

Wait and see what develops.

❦

What's brown, likes peanuts, and weighs
two tons?
A chocolate-covered elephant.

❦

What do you call a singer who's not old
enough to be a tenor?
A niner!

❦

What's black and white and red on
Christmas Eve?
Rudolph the Red-Nosed Penguin.

❦

What weighs three tons, has tusks, and
loves pepperoni pizza?
An Italian circus elephant.

❦

What's the difference between an excited
skunk and a calm skunk?
An 80-dollar laundry bill.

❦

What time is it when an elephant climbs
into your bed?
Time to get a new bed.

What's the difference between a man going up the stairs and a man looking up the stairs?
One steps up the stairs, and the other stares up the steps.

What kind of music do welders dance to?
Heavy metal.

33

A Grab-Bag of Goofies

Goofy visitor: Why does that old hog keep trying to come into my room? Is it because he likes me?

Goofy farmer: Not really, friend. You see, that's his room during the winter.

Traveler in a balloon (calling down to a farmer): Ahoy there, where am I?

Goofy farmer: Hah! You can't fool me, feller. You're right up there in that little basket.

Goofy thought about short people: *You're so short, you'd have to climb up on stepladder to kick an ant in the ankle.*

Goofy mountain climber: *Someone who wants to take a peak.*

Goofy boss: *A man who is at work early on the days you are late.*

Why is a calendar so popular?
Because it has lots of dates.

What did the goofy astronomer say when he was asked what he thought about flying saucers?
"No comet."

Sign in a goofy flower shop: Love 'em and Leave 'em.

What do they call popcorn that's too tired to pop?
Pooped corn.

Did you hear about the goofy student who thought that electricians' school was going to be easy?
He was really shocked.

Goofy optometrist: "My business is
looking better."

My goofy dog is so bad, that last week he
was expelled from obedience school.

Goofy baker: My business is doing so well
that I am rolling in the dough.

Goofy turtle salesman: "My business is
very slow."

"My business has sunk to new low," said
the goofy deep-sea diver.

Goofy Gus: Did you hear about the poet
who got arrested for writing too fast?
Goofy Guy: No, what about him?
Loony Gus: The judge took away his
poetic license.

Goofy saying: *Women who use gunpowder as
night cream end up with complexion that is
shot.*

Goofy saying: *Man who speak with forked tongue is probably a snake in the grass.*

"My business is going up," said the goofy elevator operator.

Did you hear the goofy radio announcer give the latest sports scores?

The Redskins scalped the Cowboys!
The Lions devoured the Saints!
The Vikings butchered the Dolphins!
The Chiefs massacred the Patriots!
The Falcons tore the Cardinals to shreds!
The Broncos trampled the Rams!
The Bears mauled the Buccaneers!
The Giants squashed the Packers!
The Jets shot down the Eagles!
The Bengals chewed up the Colts!

Goofy wife: Harry, let's go jogging together.
Goofy husband: Why?
Goofy wife: My doctor told me I could lose weight by working out with a dumbbell.

"My business is sick," said the goofy
  doctor.

A goofy movie star returned to his
boyhood home for the first time since he
became famous.

"I guess everyone around here talks a
lot about me," the star said to the goofy
mayor.

"That's right," agreed the goofy mayor.
"You're so famous we even put a sign in
front of your old house."

The goofy movie star beamed.
"Really?" he exclaimed. "What does the
sign say?"

Smiling broadly, the goofy mayor
replied, "It says Stop!"

34
Goofy Gathering

My goofy town is so small that the local gang boss, Mr. Big, is a midget.

My goofy boss has a heart of stone. He can even trace his roots back to a petrified forest.

My goofy secretary isn't an office gossip. She's a magician. She can turn an eyeful or an earful into a mouthful.

I'm not sure it's true, but I heard in Goofyville they hang spaghetti on Christmas trees instead of tinsel. The only problem is the meatballs don't light up.

Goofy hostess: You know, I've heard a
great deal about you.
Goofy politician: Possibly, but you can't
prove a thing.

⌐∞੭

Goofy mom: For dessert, you have your
choice of good or evil.
Goofy Lyle: What do you mean?
Goofy mom: Angel food cake or devil's
food cake.

⌐∞੭

Goofy wife: Wake up! Wake up! There's a
burglar in the kitchen and he's eating
the leftover stew we had for supper.
Goofy husband: Go back to sleep and
don't worry, dear. I'll bury him in the
morning.

⌐∞੭

Last night I slept like a goofy lawyer. First
I lied on one side, then I lied on the
other.

⌐∞੭

An angry goofy worker went into her
company's payroll office to complain
that her paycheck was $50 short.
The payroll supervisor checked the books
and said, "I see here that last week you
were overpaid by $50.

I can't recall your complaining about that."

"Well, I'm willing to overlook an occasional error, but this is two in a row," said the goofy worker.

"I really loved my vacation in California," said the goofy lady on the plane.

"Where did you stay?" the goofy man next to her asked.

"San Jose."

"Madam, in California we pronounce the J as an H. We say San Hosay. How long were you there?"

"All of hune and most of Huly."

Goofy customer: Does the manager know you knocked over this whole pile of canned tomatoes?

Goofy stock boy: I think so. He's underneath.

Once upon a time there was a goofy ventriloquist who was so bad you could see his lips move even when he wasn't saying anything.

Did you hear about the goofy fish hook
with a camera on it? It took pictures
of the fish that got away.

Goofy mother: Will you help me fix
dinner?
Gertrude: I didn't know it was broken.

Goofy boy: They call a man's wife his
better half don't they?
Goofy father: Yes, they do.
Goofy boy: Then I guess if a man marries
twice, there's nothing left of him.

Goofy Gret: Did you hear about the man
who bought a new pair of snow tires?
Goofy Gene: No, what happened?
Goofy Gret: They melted before he got
home.

35

Goofy Gems

What's the difference between a
   locomotive engineer and a school
   teacher?
*One minds the train; the other trains the
   mind.*

What has four wheels and goes honk?
A goose on a skateboard.

What is the most boring Clark Gable
   film?
Yawn with the Wind.

What do you get if you hit a gopher with
   a golf club?
A mole-in-one.

What's the difference between Peter Pan and someone who quit the bomb squad?

One doesn't want to be grown up, and the other doesn't want to be blown up.

If Fortune had a daughter, what would she be called?

Miss Fortune.

A zebra with wide stripes married a zebra with narrow stripes. Their first son had no stripes. What did they call him?

Leroy.

If you saw nine elephants walking down the street with red socks, and one elephant walking down the street with green socks, what would this prove?

That nine out of ten elephants wear red socks.

If a relative had an upset stomach, what would you call her?

Antacid.

What would you get if you crossed
poison ivy and a four-leaf clover?
A rash of good luck.

You peel the outside, boil the inside,
nibble on the outside, and throw the
inside in the garbage. What is it?
Corn on the cob.

If my brother had a split personality, who
would he be?
Your half brother.

If your aunt ran off to get married, what
would you call her?
Antelope.

What do you call a man walking around
with his hands in the air, waving a
white flag?
A goofy soldier on war maneuvers.

What happens to illegally parked frogs?
They get toad away.

What snake builds things?
A boa constructor.

What's the difference between a crazy
  hare and a counterfeit coin?
One is a mad bunny, the other is bad money.

What does a baby snake play with?
A rattle.

What is full of holes but holds water?
A sponge.

What did the gingerbread man's
  grandfather use for walking?
A candy cane.

What young outlaw was very overweight?
Belly the Kid.

What crime-fighting gardener rides a
  horse and wears a mask?
The Lawn Ranger.

What sign did the real estate agent put in front of the Old Woman Who Lived in a Shoe's house?
Soled.

What's the difference between a photocopy machine and the Hong Kong flu?
One makes facsimiles, the other sick families.

What kind of bears like to bask in the sun?
Solar bears.

What does a maple tree like to watch on TV?
Sap operas.

What is a group of goofy paratroopers called?
Air pollution.

What school do toothbrushes go to?
Colgate.

What do horses do for entertainment?
Watch stable TV.

What's a bee's favorite musical?
Stinging in the Rain.

What cartoon character lives in Jellystone
Park and eats health food?
Yogurt Bear.

What is a dog's favorite musical?
The Hound of Music.

36
A Galaxy of Goofies

The biggest social event of the season in the Goofy Pen Manufacturing Company is the "Pen Point Ball."

Goofy girl: Did you hear about the dog
    that went to the flea circus?
Goofy boy: No, what happened?
Goofy girl: He stole the show.

I work only when I'm fired. What am I?
A rocket.

It's funny, but a goofy horse eats best when it doesn't have a bit in its mouth.

Larry Goofy: My brother swallowed a box
    of firecrackers.

Louis Goofy: Is he all right now?
Larry Goofy: I don't know. We haven't
    heard the last report.

Goofy lima bean: I had a date with a
    green bean, but I only think she went
    out with me because of the money I
    spent on her.
Goofy pork n' bean: I think she's stringing
    you along.

Goofy boy: Are there any fish that are
    musical?
Goofy girl: Of course! Haven't you ever
    heard of a piano tuna?

Who screams, "The sky is falling! The sky
    is falling!" and suffers from inflation?
Henny Nickel.

I have wings but I can't fly. What am I?
A large mansion.

I have teeth but no mouth. What am I?
A comb.

I have hands and a face, but I can't touch or smile. What am I?
A clock.

I have legs but I can't walk. What am I?
A chair.

That guy is so frail and skinny that the last time someone kicked sand in his face, the grains knocked him out cold.

I lived in a tough, goofy neighborhood. On Christmas Eve I hung my stockings over the fireplace and Santa Claus stole them.

I know a goofy man who is so dumb the only thing that can stay in his head for more than a day is a cold.

Goofy girl: Wow! You are dumb. In fact, you're close to an idiot.
Goofy boy: Want me to move away from you?

You have a pretty little goofy head. For a head, it's pretty little and its goofy.

Little Gale Goofy was visiting her grandmother on the farm for the first time. One day she spotted a peacock, a bird she had never seen before. She stared at it silently for a few moments, then ran into the house crying, "Oh, Granny, come look! One of your chickens is blooming!"

What do they call a goofy hobo who's been caught in a pouring rain?
A damp tramp.

We only have two goofy things to worry about: One, that things will never get back to normal; and two, that they already have.

He is so goofy that if goofyness were gold, he'd be Fort Knox.

He's such a goofy lazy person that getting up in the morning makes him tired.

Did you hear about the goofy upside-down
lighthouse? It's for submarines.

Did you hear about the Goofy skin diver
who failed divers' school. The subjects
were just too deep for him.

37

Gregarious Goofies

Goofy George: You wouldn't hit a man with glasses, would you?

Goofy bully: Heck, no! I always use my fists.

Goofy son: I'm really glad you named me Geoff.

Goofy mother: Why?

Goofy son: That's what all the kids at school call me.

Goofy teacher: If you took three apples from a basket that contained 13 apples, how many apples would you have?

Goofy student: If you took three apples, you'd have three apples.

Did you hear about the goofy shirts and blouses with boards sewn into the seams? They're for people with poor posture.

Did you hear about the goofy gift-wrapped empty boxes? They are to give as presents to people who say, "I don't need anything."

Goofy passenger: Does this airplane fly faster than sound?

Goofy flight attendant: It certainly does.

Goofy passenger: Then would you ask the pilot to slow down? My friend and I would like to talk.

Goofy employer: And you say you've been fired from ten different jobs?

Goofy worker: Well, my father always said, "Never be a quitter!"

Can giraffes have babies?
No, they can only have giraffes.

Goofy speaker: A horrible thing has happened. I've just lost my wallet with $500 in it. I'll give $50 to anyone who will return it.

Goofy voice from the rear: I'll give $100.

A goofy elderly woman was sitting on a plane and getting increasingly nervous about the thunderstorm raging outside. She turned to a minister who was sitting next to her.

"Reverend, you are a man of God. Why can't you do something about this problem?"

The goofy minister replied: "Lady, I'm in sales, not management."

Four-year-old Goofy Gracie was visiting her grandparents. When she was put to bed, she sobbed and said she was afraid of the dark and wanted to go home.

"But you don't sleep with the light on at home, do you, darling?" asked her grandmother.

"No," replied the Goofy Gracie, "but there it's my own dark."

Goofy Grant: Why is Daddy singing so much tonight?

Goofy mother: He's trying to sing the
    baby to sleep before the babysitter
    gets here.

Goofy Grant: You know, if I were the baby,
    I'd pretend I was asleep.

Goofy boss: You're recommending Jack for
    a raise? I can't believe it—he's the
    laziest worker on the line!

Goofy foreman: Yes, but his snoring keeps
    the other workers awake!

Did you hear about the goofy preacher
who was delivering a sermon and made a
mistake? He was referring to the devil as
the father of all lawyers instead of the
father of all liars. But the error was so
insignificant he didn't bother to correct
himself.

I have a very fine goofy doctor. If you
can't afford the operation, he touches up
the X-rays.

I went to visit the doctor for my sore
foot. He said, "I'll have you walking in an
hour." He did. He stole my car.

Goofy radio anouncement: If you must
drink while you're driving home, be
sure the radio in the car is turned up
loud. That way you won't hear the
crash.

Did you hear about the goofy speach
school? They teach you how to speak
clearly. To do this, they fill your
mouth with marbles and you're
supposed to talk clearly right through
the marbles. Every day you lose one
marble. When you've lost all your
marbles . . . you're done.

The goofy doctor opened the window
wide. He said, "Stick your tongue out
the window."
I asked, "What for?"
He said, "I'm mad at my neighbors."

38

A Gala of Goofies

Who was born on a mountaintop, killed a
    bear when he was only three, and
    swims underwater?
Davy Crocodile.

Who got nervous picking pickled peppers?
P-P-P-P-P-Peter P-P-P-P-P-Piper.

Who's short, can spin gold from straw,
    and is very, very wrinkled?
Crumplestiltskin.

Who caught flies with his tongue and was
    the first treasurer of the United
    States?
Salamander Hamilton.

Who writes mystery stories and blooms
in spring?
Edgar Allan Poesy.

Who has a beard, wears a dirty white
robe, and rides a pig?
Lawrence of Arkansas.

Who trains court jesters?
Fool teachers.

Who said, "Will you please join me?"
A person who was coming apart.

Who do mice see when they get sick?
The hickory dickory doc.

How did the goofy musician break his
leg?
He fell over a clef.

How does a farmer mend his overalls?
With cabbage patches.

How did the mouse pass his final exam?
He squeaked by.

How do you make a hot dog stand?
Steal its chair.

How did Noah know how to build an Ark?
He studied arkaeology!

Goofy: How are you doing with your wood carving?
Goofier: It's coming along whittle by whittle.

How does an elephant get out of a Volkswagon?
The same way he got in.

39
Goofies with Gusto

When is it safe to pet a lion?
When it's a dandelion.

When is a basketball player like a baby?
When he dribbles.

If the goofy lady was always cold, what
would you call her?
Anti-freeze.

When is a Chinese restaurant successful?
When it makes a fortune, cookie.

When does it get noisy in a magazine
store?
When Time marches on.

Where do goofy bunny rabbits like to
spend their vacations?
On Easter Island.

Where do pencils come from?
Pennsylvania.

Where should proofreaders work?
In a house of correction.

Where should you go if you lose your
fish?
The lost-and-flounder department.

Where do millionaires work out?
At wealth clubs.

Where's one place you can always find
money?
In the dictionary, of course!

Where do jellyfish get their jelly?
From ocean currents.

Where does Santa stay overnight when
   he travels?
At ho-ho-hotels.

Where do you find chili beans?
At the North Pole.

40
Guaranteed to Be Goofy

Why do dressmakers like the wide-open
   spaces?
So they don't feel hemmed in.

Why were the sardines out of work?
Because they got canned.

Why do tigers have stripes?
Because they'd look funny in polka dots.

Why was the goofy woman always able to
   remember the names of people under
   five feet tall?
Because she had a short memory.

Why do you occasionally see goofy people pushing a house down the street?
That's how they jump-start their furnaces.

Why did the prizefighter like his new job?
He got to punch the time clock.

Why did the goofy girl buy a new garbage can?
She wanted to enter the Mess America contest.

Why couldn't the goofy boy see his bicycle after he parked it behind a tree?
Because the bark was bigger than his bike.

Goofy guy: Why don't astronauts get hungry in outer space?
Goofy gal: I don't know, why?
Goofy guy: Because they just had a big launch!

Why were the boats all docked in a
    straight line?
Because they were rowboats.

Why was the loaf of bread full of holes?
Because it was hole wheat.

Why are spiders good baseball players?
Because they know how to catch flies.

Why did the moth eat a hole in the rug?
Because it wanted to see the floor show.

Why don't they make astronauts out of
    elephants?
*Because space helmets aren't big enough to fit
    them.*

Why did the hippo need to use soap?
Because he left a ring around the river.

Why is a schoolyard larger at recess?
Because there are more feet in it.

How do you get a one-armed goofy man
    out of a tree?
Wave.

Goofy Gus: Don't you ever peel the
    banana before eating it?
Goofy Gabe: No. I already know what's inside.

    The goofy football team—nicknamed
the Blockheads—no longer gets ice water.
The player with the recipe graduated.

    Did you hear about the goofy man
who locked his keys in the car? It took
him nine hours to get his family out.

How do you make a goofy shish kebab?
Shoot an arrow into a garbage can.

    The goofy boy was so big that he
could only play seek.

Why did the goofy man put a diaper on
    his clock?
Because he heard times were changing.

Why did the goofy woman tiptoe quietly past her medicine cabinet?
Because she didn't want to wake her sleeping pills.

What do they call anyone with an IQ of 50 in Goofyville?
Gifted.

Did you hear that they had to close down the Goofyville Library?
Somebody stole the book.

Why do goofy people drink less Kool-Aid than other folks?
Because they have a hard time getting two quarts of water into that little envelope.

If a goofy man and a goofy woman jumped off a 40-story building, who would land first?
The goofy man because the goofy woman would have to stop and ask for directions.

Why is Santa Claus goofy?
*Who else would wear a red suit during the
    holidays?*

How can you tell where a rich flamingo
    lives?
By the wrought-iron goofies on the front lawn.

41

Goofy Definitions

Aquaintance: A person you know well enough to borrow money from—but not well enough to lend money to.

Airplanes: The world's leading cause of white knuckles.

Amiss: Someone who is not married.

Blind date: When you expect to meet a vision, and she turns out to be a sight.

Bore: A person who insists upon talking about himself when you want to talk about yourself.

Boredom: A state of mind that usually ends
   when school lets out.

Childish Games: Those at which your wife
   beats you.

Cost plus: Expensive.

Claustrophobia: Fear of Santa.

Dog sled: Polar coaster.

Flood: A river too big for its bridges.

Flashlight: A case to carry dead batteries
   in.

Gossip: Good memory with a tongue hung
   in the middle of it.

Highborn: Anybody born on top of a
   mountain.

Iceberg: A kind of permanent wave.

Little Leaguer: Peanut batter.

Peanut Butter: A bread spread.

Stationery Store: A store that pretty much stays at the same location.

Screens: An invention for keeping flies in the house.

Trapeze Artist: Someone who gets the hang of things.

Traffic Light: A little green light that changes to red as your car approaches.

Zoo: A place where animals look at silly people.

42
Goofy Waiters

Diner: Waiter, I'm so hungry I could eat a horse!

Goofy waiter: You certainly came to the right place.

Diner: Waiter, I'm in a hurry. Will the griddle cakes be long?

Goofy waiter: No, sir, they'll all be round.

Diner: Waiter, this steak is rare. Didn't you hear me say "well done"?

Goofy waiter: Yes, sir. Thank you, sir!

Diner: Do you have lobster tails?

Goofy waiter: Certainly, sir: Once upon a time, there was a little lobster . . .

Diner: Waiter, there's a fly in my soup!
Goofy waiter: That's funny, there were two
of them when I left the kitchen.

Diner: Waiter, isn't this toast burnt?
Goofy waiter: No, sir, it just fell on the
floor.

Diner: Waiter, there's a fly in my soup!
Goofy waiter: Don't worry, the frog should
snap it up any second now.

Diner: Waiter, do you serve crabs here?
Goofy waiter: We serve anyone; sit down.

43

More Goofy Knock-Knocks

Knock, knock.
Who's there?
Chester.
Chester who?
Chester minute and I'll see.

Knock, knock.
Who's there?
Desdemona.
Desdemona who?
Desdemona Lisa still hang on the gallery wall?

Knock, knock.
Who's there?
Jewel.
Jewel who?
Jewel know who when you open the door.

Knock, knock.
Who's there?
Anita Loos.
Anita Loos who?
Anita Loos about 20 pounds.

Knock, knock.
Who's there.
Ghana.
Ghana who?
"Ghana wash that man right out of my
      hair."

Knock, knock.
Who's there?
Gil.
Gil who?
Gil the umpire!

Knock, knock.
Who's there?
Just Diane.
Just Diane who?
Just Diane to see you.

Will you remember me in five years?

Yes.
Will you remember me next year?
Yes.
Will you remember me next month?
Yes.
Will you remember me next week?
Yes.
Will you remember me tomorrow?
Yes.
Will you remember me in another
  minute?
Yes.
Will you remember me in another second?
Yes.
Knock, knock.
Who's there?
You forgot me already?

Knock, knock.
Who's there?
Sensuous.
Sensuous who?
Sensuous such a nice person, I wish you a
  happy life.

Knock, knock.
Who's there?
Dawn.
Dawn who?
Dawnkey. Hee haw.

Knock, knock.
Who's there?
Uganda.
Uganda who?
Uganda come in without knocking!

44

Goodness Gracious! More Goofy Knock-Knocks

Knock, knock.
Who's there?
Amarillo.
Amarillo who?
Amarillo-fashioned cowboy.

Knock, knock.
Who's there?
Eskimo, Christian, Italian.
Eskimo, Christian, Italian who?
Eskimo, Christian, Italian no lies.

Knock, knock.
Who's there?
Ether.
Ether who?

Ether Bunny.

Knock, knock.
Who's there?
Stella.
Stella who?
Stella nother Ether Bunny.

Knock, Knock.
Who's there?
Samoa.
Samoa who?
Samoa Ether Bunnies.

Knock, knock.
Who's there?
Alby.
Alby who?
Alby glad when school's over.

Knock, knock.
Who's there?
Duncan.
Duncan who?
Duncan doughnuts in your milk makes
    'em soft.

Knock, knock.
Who's there?
Amos.
Amos who?
Amos-kito bit me.

Knock, knock.
Who's there?
Andy.
Andy who?
Andy bit me again.

Knock, knock.
Who's there?
Apollo.
Apollo who?
Apollo you anywhere if you'll blow in
    my ear.

Knock, knock.
Who's there?
Sari.
Sari, who?
Sari I was sarong!